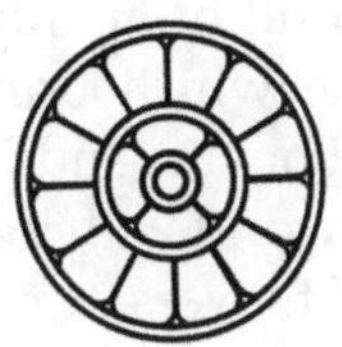

THE TEACHINGS OF FLOWERS

THE LIFE AND WORK OF THE MOTHER
OF THE SRI AUROBINDO ASHRAM

Impressum

Acknowledgments: The Mother of the Sri Aurobindo Ashram was a beloved teacher and guide for thousands of people. She worked with Sri Aurobindo for the manifestation of a new consciousness which brings the changes that people experience all over the world today. Their work and teachings open pathways of progress for all humanity. This book comes from a video of the same title which brings the Mother's flower teachings in the context of her life and work. The Mother's work links our visible, tangible world with inner worlds using the true meanings and qualities of flowers.

Quotations from The Mother and Sri Aurobindo's writings are protected by the copyright of the Sri Aurobindo Ashram Trust, Pondicherry, India.

First Edition 2011
Second Editon 2022
The Teachings of Flowers
(The Life and Work of the Mother of the Sri Aurobindo Ashram)
Loretta Shartsis

ISBN 978-93-95460-04-0 (print)
ISBN 978-93-95460-05-7 (ebook)

BISAC Code:
OCC026000, BODY, MIND & SPIRIT / Yoga see HEALTH & FITNESS / Yoga
REF019000, REFERENCE / Quotations
DES007000, DESIGN / Graphic Arts / General

Thema Subject Category:
AKLB, Illustration
VX, Mind, body, spirit

Cataloging-in-Publication Data for this title is available from the Library of Congress.

Printed and bound in India by:
PRISMA, Aurelec/ Prayogshala,
Auroville 605101, Tamil Nadu, India

Digital Editions produced by:
DMI Systems Pvt Ltd, Vishnupuri,
Aligarh 202001, Uttar Pradesh, India

Published by PRISMA, an imprint of Digital Media Initiatives
www.prisma.haus, www.dmi.systems

*Flowers speak to us
when we know how to listen*

The Mother

INTRODUCTION

The Mother of the Sri Aurobindo Ashram was a beloved teacher and guide for thousands of people. She worked with Sri Aurobindo for the manifestation of a new consciousness which brings the changes that people experience all over the world today. Their work and teachings open pathways of progress for all humanity.

This book comes from a video of the same title which brings the Mother's flower teachings in the context of her life and work. The Mother's work links our visible, tangible world with inner worlds using the true meanings and qualities of flowers.

We now know that the earth is formed from the dust of the stars in the nebulae of our cosmos, and we are made of the substance of the earth. The Mother taught that the dreams of creation live in flowers as a force and vibration which we share, and she used the true essence of flowers as a spiritual teaching. We share our aspirations for progress with the earth.

In the evolution of the earth, each flower has some particular quality which we have, or want to have, because people and flowers alike are children of the earth and stars.

The facts and incidences of the Mother's life come from various histories and personnel stories. All quotations from the Mother are marked with her symbol. ❋ All quotations from Sri Aurobindo are marked with his symbol. ✡ References giving the source of each quotation are at the back of the book.

"Be like a flower. One must try to become like a flower: open, frank, equal, generous and kind….

A flower is open to all that surrounds it: Nature, light, the rays of the sun, the wind. It exerts a specific influence on all those around it. It radiates a joy and a beauty.

A flower is frank; it hides nothing of its beauty, and lets it flow frankly out of itself. What is within, what it has deep within, it lets come out, so that everyone can see it.

A flower is equal; it has no preference. Everyone can enjoy its beauty and its perfume without rivalry. It is equal and the same for everybody. There is no difference or anything whatsoever.

A flower is generous; without reserve or restriction how it gives the mysterious beauty and the very perfume of Nature. It sacrifices itself entirely for our pleasure. Even its life it sacrifices to express this beauty and the secret of the things gathered within itself.

A flower is kind; it has such a tenderness, it is so sweet, so close to us, so loving. Its presence fills us with joy. it is always cheerful and happy.

Happy is he who can exchange his qualities with the real qualities of the flowers. Try to cultivate in yourself their refined qualities.

When I give flowers, it is as an answer to the aspiration coming from the very depths of your being. It is an aspiration or a need – it depends upon the person. It may fill a void, or else give you the impetus to progress, or it may help you to find the inner harmony to establish peace.

I give you flowers so that you may develop the Divine qualities they symbolize. And they can directly transmit into your soul all that they contain, pure, unalloyed. They possess a very subtle and very deep power and influence.

Now it seems to me that you wish to become like a flower, or to cultivate these qualities. And, you know, each flower symbolizes an aspect, an emanation, an aspiration, and a progress in the evolution of the earth." ⊛

These are the words of the Mother of the Sri Aurobindo Ashram in Pondicherry, India. She used our similarities with the earth in her spiritual teaching. We know now that our earth is made of the dust of the stars from the nebulae in our cosmos. And we are made of the earth. Everything that we see, all that we have, everything that we are comes from the substance of the earth.

So we, too, are made of the dust of the stars. As the world we live in evolves through the unfolding of time, our progress is part of the evolution of our earth. In the evolution of our earth, each flower has some particular quality which we have, or want to have, because people and flowers alike are children of the earth and stars.

Throughout the ages, mankind has gone to Nature for fulfillment, for peace, for renewal. When the Mother saw that the dreams of creation live in a flower as a force and vibration which we share, she used the true meaning of flowers as a spiritual teaching, to guide people and to help them to progress.

The Mother showed us that each flower is a Mantra. A "Mantra" is a word, which, in itself, is the living consciousness and force of the meaning it expresses. Proper use of a mantra can change things. Each flower has a living vibration we can receive. Flowers have much to give us. The Mother compared the aspiration of a forest to our own aspiration for light.

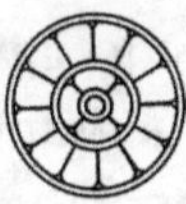

"Have you never watched a forest, with all its countless trees and plants simply struggling to catch the light – twisting and trying in a hundred possible ways just to be in the sun? That is precisely the feeling in the physical consciousness – the urge, the movement, the push towards the light.

Plants have more of it in their being than men. Their whole life is a worship of light.

Light is, of course, the material symbol of the Divine – and the sun represents, under material conditions, the Supreme Consciousness.

The plants have felt it quite distinctly in their own simple, blind way. Their aspiration is intense, if you know how to become aware of it."

Flowers became part of the Mother's work and teachings around the time she was twenty-five years old. In later years she spoke about the time she first learned how to use flowers.

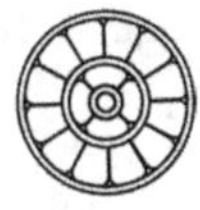

"All the flowers to which I have given a significance receive exactly the force which I put into them and transmit it. People don't always receive it because most of the time they are less receptive than the flower, and they waste the force that has been put in it through their lack of consciousness and receptivity. But the force is there and the flower receives it wonderfully. I knew this a long time ago. ....Fifty years ago.

There was an occultist who gave me lessons in occultism for two years. His wife was a wonderful clairvoyant and had an absolutely remarkable capacity - precisely - of transmitting forces. They lived in Tlemcen, Algeria. I was living in Paris. I used to correspond with them. I had not yet met them at all. And then, one day she sent me, in a letter, petals of the pomegranate flower, which carry the vibration of the "Divine's Love". At that time I had not given the meaning to the flower. Divine Love is the vibration of love that is at the origin of all love and fills the universe. She sent me petals of the pomegranate flower telling me that these petals were bringing me her protection and force.

Now, at that time I used to wear my watch on a chain. Wrist watches were not known then, or there were very few. And there was also a small eighteenth century magnifying-glass...it was quite small. And it had two lenses, you see, like all reading glasses; there were two lenses mounted on a small golden frame, and it was hanging from my chain. Now, between the two glasses I put these petals, and I used to carry this about with me always, because I wanted to keep it with me; you see, I trusted this lady and knew she had power. I wanted to keep this with me, and I always felt a kind of energy, warmth, confidence, force which came from that thing....I did not think about it, you see, but I felt it like that.

And then, one day, suddenly I felt quite depleted, as though a support that was there had gone; something very unpleasant. I said, "It is strange, what has happened? Nothing really unpleasant has happened to me. Why do I feel like this, so empty, emptied of energy?" And in the evening, when I took off my watch and chain, I noticed that one of the small glasses had come off and all the petals were gone. There was not one petal left. Then I really knew that they carried a considerable charge of power, for I had felt the difference without even knowing the reason. I didn't know the reason and it had made a considerable difference. So it was after this that I saw how one could use flowers by charging them with forces. They are extremely receptive." ⊛

The Mother was born into a wealthy Paris family on February 21, 1878. Her name was Mirra Alfassa. Her initials were "M A", MA. Mirra would be called "The Mother", or "Ma" for most of her adult life. Mother, or Ma, in the spiritual traditions of many cultures means a realized being, a person who has realized the infinite, eternal source of the creation and the totality of its manifestation. Mirra's family did not know the spiritual meaning of the word MA, but the two letters of her spiritual title were embroidered on her baby clothes and blankets from the very beginning of her life.

The Mother was always conscious. She began to practice yoga when she was four years old. There was a small chair in her bedroom, and sat in meditation for hours. A brilliant light descended above her head, causing activity in her brain. She wanted to unite with the light. At age four, she knew she was going to do a great work, something as yet unknown on earth. In later years she spoke about the longing for light in the forest.

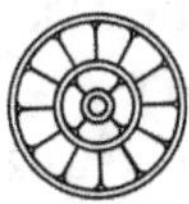

"The movement of love is not limited to human beings and it is perhaps less distorted in other worlds than the human.

Look at the flowers and trees. When the sun sets and all becomes silent, sit down for a moment and put yourself into communion with nature; you will feel rising from the earth, from below the roots of the trees, and mounting upwards and coursing through their fibres, up to the highest outstretching branches, an aspiration of an intense love and longing, - a longing for something that brings light and gives happiness, for the light is gone and they wish to have it back again.

There is a yearning so pure and intense that if you can feel the movement in the trees, your own being will go up in an ardent prayer for the peace and light and love that are unmanifested here." ⊛

By the age of five, the Mother understood that in order to become a true individual, she had to consciously unify her being around her own divine center. Without any guidance she started to create a process which she would eventually teach to people from all over the world.

All during her childhood, the Mother was conscious of a more-than-human force and light above her head. It often entered into her body and worked there in a supernatural way. She was aware that this force was one with her own secret being. As she was growing up, she sometimes exhibited supernatural strength and brilliance and went into superconscious trance.

Between the ages of 11 and 13, she remained conscious at night. While her body was asleep, she went out of her body to help suffering people. She also had a series of experiences which revealed the existence of God, and man's possibility of uniting with God, and of realizing him integrally in daily life.

During the night, she was given a discipline for the fulfillment of the realization of this divine consciousness by several teachers, some of whom she later met. Her relationship with one teacher continued to increase. It was Sri Aurobindo. Although she didn't know anything about Indian philosophies or religions, she called him Krishna. She understood that one day they would work together to bring to others the light and consciousness that she experienced.

At the age of 12, because of her inner experiences, the Mother gained knowledge and mastery over the secret powers and processes of nature. With these subtle powers she could understand the true essence of a flower. Later in life she explained how she could understand a flower's real meaning.

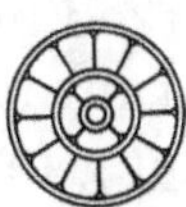

"Each flower has its own special significance, but not as we understand it mentally. There is a mental projection when one gives a precise meaning to a flower. It may answer, it may vibrate to the touch of this projection, and it may accept the meaning, but a flower has no equivalent of the mental consciousness.

In the vegetable kingdom there is the beginning of the soul, but there is no beginning of the mental consciousness.

In animals it is different, mental life begins to form, and for them, things have a meaning. But in flowers it is rather like the movement of a little baby – it is neither a sensation nor a feeling, but something of both; it is a spontaneous movement, a very special vibration. So if one is in contact with it, if one feels it, one gets an impression which may be translated by a thought.

That is how I have given a meaning to flowers and plants – there is a kind of identification with the vibration, a perception of the quality it represents. Sometimes it comes suddenly, occasionally it takes time, but little by little, through a kind of approximation, there is a coming together of these vibrations, which are of a vital-emotional order, and the vibration of the mental thought, and if there is a sufficient harmony, one has a direct perception of what the plant may signify."

As she grew up, the Mother followed her spiritual path without any help. She saw that the new consciousness would be the next step in human evolution, and it would come more quickly if people worked on themselves. Realization of higher consciousness had always been the goal of spiritual seekers, but now it was going to manifest in humanity on a wide scale. Between the ages of 19 and 20 she attained a conscious union with this Divine Presence. In teaching, she used a tree to explain the difference between having our usual consciousness and having the Divine Consciousness.

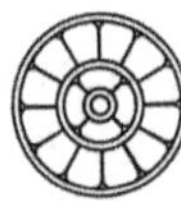

"Consciousness is the faculty of becoming aware of anything through identification with it. But mere awareness is not knowledge. Only when the consciousness participates in the divine consciousness does it get full knowledge by identification with the object. When the divine consciousness identifies with an object, it knows it thoroughly, because it always becomes one with the essential truth or law behind each fact.

For example, if you identify yourself with a tree, you become aware in the way that a tree is aware of itself, yet you do not come to know everything about a tree for the simple reason that it, itself, is not possessed of such knowledge. You do share the tree's inner feeling, but you certainly do not understand the truth it stands for any more than by being conscious of your own, natural self you possess at once the divine reality which you secretly are.

Whereas, if you are one with the divine consciousness you know – over and above how the tree feels – what the truth behind it is. In short, you know everything because the divine consciousness knows everything."

The Mother was part of the great art movement of French Impressionism. She was painted and drawn by some of the Impressionists. With her deep love of beauty, she also became an artist at that time. In 1914 she came to India to meet Sri Aurobindo. She recognized him immediately. When they met, they both knew that the work of bringing this new consciousness for mankind would be successful. Because of the outbreak of World War I in 1914, the Mother had to return to France. A year later she went to Japan, where she continued her inner work until 1920, when she returned to India, to live and work with Sri Aurobindo.

The Mother said that one must go into the depths or heights of creation which have never been manifested upon earth and become conscious of this in order to manifest it on earth. Up to that time, these states of being were not conscious in man. The work to be done was to get identified with them, and then bring them into the outer consciousness and manifest them in action. Sri Aurobindo called that consciousness "Supramental" because the mind is the height of human evolution, and to receive and keep this new consciousness, mankind had to develop beyond the mind.

Realization of the heights or depths of creation is the goal. The Mother spoke of the basis, the means, and the goal of realization for the individual, the collectivity and the earth.

"Sincerity is the basis of true realization. It is the means, the path - and it is also the goal. There is a marvelous joy in being sincere. Every act of sincerity carries in itself its own reward: the feeling of purification, of soaring upwards, of liberation one gets when one has rejected even the tiniest particle of falsehood.

To be perfectly sincere one must be free from all preferences and judgements.

Sincerity is the safeguard, the protection, the guide, and finally the transforming power.

If we are to be total and complete beings, to have an integral realization, we should be able to express our spiritual experience mentally, vitally, physically. And the more our expression is perfect, executed by a complete and perfect being, the more integral will our realization be.

We may say that perfection may be attained in the individual, the collectivity, on the earth and in the universe when, at every moment the receptivity will be equal in quality and quantity to the Force which wants to manifest.

That is the supreme equilibrium.

Hence there must be a perfect equilibrium between what comes from above and what answers from below, and when the two meet, that is perfect equilibrium, which is the Realisation - a realization in constant progress." ❁

The Mother and Sri Aurobindo worked all their lives for the betterment of humanity and the earth. All over the world today people experience the rapid changes which Sri Aurobindo and Mother saw coming a hundred years ago.

People of all ages and cultures are becoming aware that something new is happening, and they want to work for growth and change. The ancient spiritual teachings of many cultures are becoming available everywhere, and people are actively seeking a change in their consciousness.

Sri Aurobindo was born in Calcutta on August 15th, 1872. He received his entire education in England. His spiritual experiences and realizations began when he returned to India in 1893.

At age 16, he took the firm decision to liberate India. On his return, at age 21, he was fully involved in India's freedom. He became one of the leading forces in the movement for India's release from British rule. In 1907-1908 he realized Nirvana, the spaceless, timeless consciousness which supports and manifests the universe. In May, 1908 the British arrested him. During his year in jail he attained Cosmic Consciousness, seeing the Divine in all beings and all things. In one of his poems, called "Form", he speaks of the consciousness in all things and all beings.

FORM

O worshipper of the formless Infinite,
   Reject not form, what dwells in it is He.
   Each finite is that deep Infinity
Enshrining His veiled soul of pure delight.
    Form in its heart of silence recondite
    Hides the significance of His mystery,
Form is the wonder-house of eternity,
A cavern of the deathless Eremite.

There is a beauty in the depths of God,
    There is a miracle of the Marvellous
      That builds the universe for its abode.
Bursting into shape and colour like a rose,
    The One, in His glory multitudinous,
      Compels the great world-petals to unclose.

Sri Aurobindo was acquitted of the charges against him in May, 1909, and he returned to revolutionary work. Several great men led India to freedom, but in mid-1909 it was Sri Aurobindo who single-handedly carried on the leadership of the free-India movement.

In 1910, Sri Aurobindo went to Pondicherry, a French Enclave in South India. He took the decision to stop his political activity and to devote himself completely to the realization and manifestation of the new consciousness.

People have been reading Sri Aurobindo's writings for over a hundred years. The Mother's teachings have been transcribed and published in books since 1931. Sri Aurobindo and the Mother explain the manifest and unmanifest creation and the influx of the new consciousness in detail. They are not just teaching philosophy, they are giving their own experiences and their books radiate their consciousness. Sri Aurobindo was a prolific writer and a great poet. His realizations come to the reader through his poetry. In a poem called "Because Thou Art", he spoke to the divine consciousness.

BECAUSE THOU ART

Because Thou art All-beauty and All-bliss,
    My soul blind and enamoured yearns for Thee;
It bears Thy mystic touch in all that is
    And thrills with the burden of that ecstasy.

Behind all eyes I meet Thy secret gaze
    And in each voice I hear Thy magic tune:
Thy sweetness hunts my heart through Nature's ways;
    Nowhere it beats now from Thy snare immune.
It loves Thy body in all living things;

Thy joy is there in every leaf and stone:
The moments bring Thee on their fiery wings;
Sight's endless artistry is Thou alone.

Time voyages with Thee upon its prow,—
And all the future's passionate hope is Thou 

Along with bringing the new consciousness, the Mother
and Sri Aurobindo taught that it would change every aspect
of our beings, and that its realization had to go all the way
into the cells of our physical body. They gave methods and
guidance and support to the increasing numbers of people
who aspired to the full realization of the consciousness that
was dawning. They taught that for this to be possible, our
physical bodies must be transformed. To do this, the body
must become more receptive to the new consciousness and
more plastic to its workings. The Mother saw that a certain
flower carried the vibration of aspiration in the physical for
Divine Love, and she used it to teach a method.

"Here is the flower we have called "Aspiration in the
Physical for the Divine's Love." By the "Physical" I mean the
physical consciousness, the most ordinary outward-going
consciousness, the normal consciousness of most human
beings, which sets such great store by comfort, good food,
good clothes, happy relationships, etc., instead of aspiring for
the higher things. Aspiration in the physical for the Divine's
Love implies that the physical asks for nothing else save that
it should feel how the Divine loves it. It realizes that all its
usual satisfactions are utterly insufficient. But there cannot be

a compromise: if the physical wants the Divine's Love it must want that alone and not say, "I shall have the Divine's Love and at the same time keep my other attachments, needs and enjoyments ..."

The fundamental seat of aspiration from which it radiates or manifests in one part of the being or another is the soul centre. When I speak of aspiration in the physical I mean that the very consciousness in you which hankers after material comfort and well-being should of itself, without being compelled by the higher parts of your nature, ask exclusively for the Divine's Love. Usually you have to show it the Light by means of your higher parts; surely this has to be done persistently, otherwise the physical would never learn and it would take Nature's common round of ages before it learns by itself. Indeed the round of Nature is intended to show it all possible sorts of satisfactions and by exhausting them convince it that none of them can really satisfy it and that what it is at bottom seeking is a divine satisfaction.

In Yoga we hasten this slow process of Nature and insist on the physical consciousness seeing the truth and learning to recognise and want it. But how to show it the truth? Well, just as you bring a light into a dark room, illumine the darkness of your physical consciousness with the intuition and aspiration of your more refined parts and keep on doing so till it realises how futile and unsatisfactory is its hunger for the low ordinary things, and turns spontaneously towards the truth. When it does turn, your whole life will be changed — the experience is unmistakable." ✸

In the 1920's, spiritual seekers from India and abroad came to Sri Aurobindo for guidance, and the Sri Aurobindo Ashram began to form. In 1926, Sri Aurobindo succeeded in establishing in himself the consciousness which would be the stable base for the new, descending supramental conscousness. In order to progress more quickly, he withdrew completely from outer life, but he still remained available to the disciples. Although they could no longer see him, they could write to him for guidance in their own inner work.

The whole material and spiritual charge of the Ashram passed to the Mother. Sri Aurobindo concentrated on the inner work, and the Mother organized the Ashram and took care of the new Ashramites. The Mother said that beauty was the presence of the Divine in the physical. Sri Aurobindo helped many Ashramites to become poets. The Mother helped artists. Sometimes she made quick sketches of people's faces, or drew a self-portrait. The Mother's love of beauty filled the atmosphere. People painted and embroidered beautiful flowers on cloth to give to her. The Ashram blossomed in all the arts. Poetry, music, drama, dance, drawing and painting were all part of the efforts to live in the divine presence which filled Sri Aurobindo's poetry.

DIVINE SIGHT

Each sight is now immortal with Thy bliss:
    My soul through the rapt eyes has come to see;
A veil is rent and they no more can miss
    The miracle of Thy world-epiphany.

Into an ecstasy of vision caught
    Each natural object is of Thee a part,
A rapture-symbol from Thy substance wrought,
    A poem shaped in Beauty's living heart,
A master-work of colour and design,
    A mighty sweetness borne on grandeur's wings;
A burdened wonder of significant line
    Reveals itself in even commonest things.

All forms are Thy dream-dialect of delight,
    O Absolute, O vivid Infinite.

The hearts of the Ashramites opened in response to the love they felt coming from Sri Aurobindo and the Mother. The Mother worked closely with them, so that with her contact and help they would be able to receive and assimilate everything they were capable of. People speak of her transcendent beauty and bliss they felt in her presence.

The Mother often used flowers to guide and help the Ashramites. She explained how flowers could be used as a living Mantra and a silent means of communication.

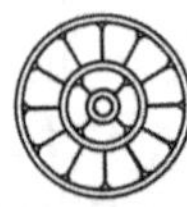

"You can easily make a speech using flowers. For instance, I have noticed that this can effectively replace the ambiguous phraseology of the ancient initiations, or the old Vedic images, which no longer hold meaning for us. Flower language is much better because it contains the Force and is extremely plastic - since it is not formulated in words, each one is free to arrange and receive it according to his own capacity. You can make long speeches using flowers."

The Ashram schedule included daily Pranam to the Mother. "Pranam" means to open oneself by bowing in reverence, love and respect in order to receive something from the higher consciousness of the guru.

The Mother gave whatever spiritual help each person was able to receive in the daily pranam.. In 1926, Pranam included sitting in meditation with the Mother and time to speak with her. By November, 1928, there were about 80 Ashramites. The Mother came to a downstairs room about 6:30 in the morning. A raised seat with a velvet covering was placed for her, and beside it was a small table with a tray full of flowers. The Ashramites approached one by one and she placed her hand on top of their head in blessing. People had very strong experiences from seeing the Mother and from her touch. After blessing, the Mother would select a particular flower and charge it with force to help each person realize the thing the flower stood for.

Pranam changed in 1938. The Mother received people one by one, standing in a small room. This gave them a private place to speak with her and to receive her help. The Mother did this for 12 years. More and more people came, and Pranam lasted for hours.

By the 1950's, there were several hundred Ashramites and the Mother could no longer speak with everyone. She came downstairs for Pranam between 9:00 and 11:00 every morning and sat in the meditation room in a high-backed chair. The Ashramites came before her in a line to receive flowers from her.

This morning Pranam gave everyone their daily contact with the Mother. It was their chance to see her, and to receive everything they could absorb from her presence. They could tell her anything that was in their hearts. It was their opportunity to ask for help, or to request a special blessing. But now they had to speak about something deeply personal in a room full of the people that they saw every day.

So when someone wanted to tell Mother something that would not be overheard by the people near by, they took specific flowers. When they gave these flowers to the Mother, she understood their personal need, and in reply she chose certain flowers from the tray on the small table next to her chair, and gave those flowers to the person standing before her. Thus the question was put and the answer was received using only flowers.

Some people wrote regularly to the Mother, asking for help. They wrote about their problems, and described their dreams and experiences. Very often, when that person came in front of the Mother for Pranam, she would catch their hand, and they knew that Mother wanted to stop them from moving on. She would give a very understanding smile, and she would pick and choose certain flowers from her tray and give them to the person one by one. It was the answer to their letter. No words were needed. Giving flowers took care of all communication, help and blessing.

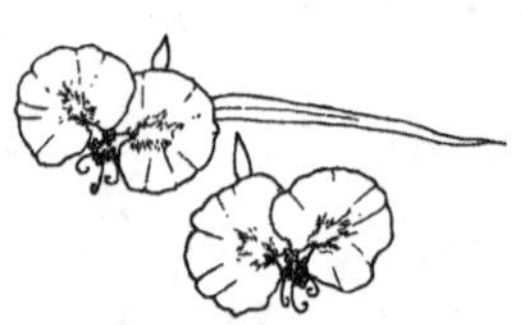

The Mother created the Ashram Departments to take care of daily needs and to support the growing spiritual community. She used her own money to pay bills, and worked on the material plane and on the inner planes to create a place where people could work on themselves to receive the new consciousness.   She was a great teacher and a tremendous organizer, tirelessly seeing to every detail of the care of the Ashramites and the Ashram.

In 1932, the Mother started going out onto the balcony at the back of the Ashram early in the morning, and soon everyone gathered in the street below her balcony for what came to be known as Mother's "Balcony Darshan". A new daily contact with the Mother opened on a wider scale. She would look at each person separately to do her inner work in them, and they would feel her conscious force. Although hundreds of people gathered each day, if someone did not come, she would later ask them why they missed the morning Darshan. Balcony Darshan continued for thirty years, until 1962.

The Mother had a room for her personal use, but she did not have a bedroom. Just as she was active at night when she was eleven years old, her consciousness did not sleep. She saw people until 2:00 in the morning. Then she reclined on her couch for two hours in the salon where she and Sri Aurobindo worked during the day. During those two hours, while her physical body rested, she went out to see people in her subtle body. Many people remember these nightly contacts. At 4:00 in the morning, she started seeing people again. Her tender care and infinite compassion included the flowers which were everywhere in the Ashram.

People in the Ashram were always interested in flowers, and the Ashram courtyards were always full of flowers. Many people came for the Mother's blessing; to receive flowers from her. And people always brought her flowers.

Once a visitor asked an Ashram gardener for a nice rose which he wanted to offer to the Mother later that afternoon. It was about 2:00. The gardener was growing some roses in pots on one of the terraces inside the Ashram compound. He went up the stairs and stretched out his hand to cut a nice rose for the visitor to take to the Mother.

The Mother was then passing through a closed corridor on the other side, and there was no way for her to see the gardener. Suddenly she started walking very fast and reached the open terrace directly across the courtyard from where the rose was growing. From there, just in time, she called out; "Don't cut, don't cut". The gardener was taken aback and, of course, stopped at once.

Later the Mother explained, "The soul of the flower came to me to be saved". She said that flowers should only be cut in the morning or evening. If they are cut or plucked during the hot hours they suffer.

Filled with the love and the consciousness of these two realized beings, the Sri Aurobindo Ashram was a living laboratory for consciousness and change. The Mother explained that we would receive the new consciousness more quickly if we realized our own soul, because our soul is the most conscious part of us. She used a flower she called "Concentration" to teach about the individual soul and the impersonal Self behind the soul.

"Here is concentration; to concentrate for developing the intelligence, for developing the inborn faculties which are hidden within ourselves.

To concentrate means to find oneself. It is the quest, the means to follow. It is the shortest way to get anything. One has only to concentrate – but deep within – and toc! you get the thing, or the word, the idea, the feeling, the place you want to discover, the plane of consciousness, and with perseverance and a constant effort, find the Self, and the individual soul – to concentrate in order to find the soul. With the help of concentration, one can achieve everything.

But one has to know how to concentrate, and each plane of the being has a certain level of concentration. To know how to concentrate is to acquire the power to withdraw from all other things except the one thing you wish to achieve.

Then, if one learns how to concentrate even more, really concentrate with intensity, one perceives that it is not oneself who is concentrating, and the ego does not exist any longer, but that an altogether detached will – without thoughts, unflickering, a sort of emptiness, but well sustained by the aspiration – is acting through the so-called individual self. For the Self seems to be hidden, but the concentration is well directed, deeply fixed there, within the soul-center, undisturbed by the outward happenings, discovering regions of happiness where divine sweetness reigns." ⊛

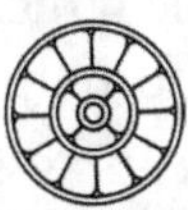

The best way of opening yourself to the profound influence of flowers is to love them. If you can have a soul-contact with them, that would be perfect. Love of flowers is a valuable help in finding and uniting with your own soul.

When you are receptive to the vibration of the soul in flowers, it puts you in a more intimate contact with your individual soul.

When you are in conscious contact with your own soul, you become aware of the impersonal soul behind the whole creation, and then, through this, you can enter into contact with flowers and know the soul prayer that they represent.

The impersonal soul is the region in the creation which does not belong to any individual in particular – the region of the soul which is in the creation as air is in the atmosphere.

Perhaps the beauty of the flowers is also a means used by nature itself to awaken in human beings the attraction of the soul. ⊛

When people came to see the Mother, she gave them flower petals which she charged with consciousness. The Ashramites made small envelopes, two inches by two and a half inches in size, to hold the delicate flower petals. These came to be known as "Blessing Packets". People received miraculous help from these flower petals which the Mother filled with the force of her consciousness to help and protect them. People asked her about the sense of beauty in the flowers. With so much love for flowers, people wanted to know if the flowers loved.

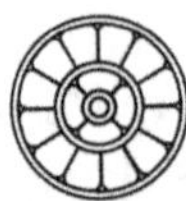

"Do flowers have a sense of beauty? Yes, flowers do have a sense of beauty. As soon as organic life comes into manifestation, the vital element comes in, and it is this vital element which gives to flowers their sense of beauty. It is not perhaps individualized in the sense we understand it, but it is the sense of the species, and the species always tries to realize it.

I have noticed a first rudiment of the soul presence and vibration in vegetal life, and truly, this blossoming one calls a flower is the first manifestation of the presence of the soul. The soul is individualized only in man, but it was there before him; however, it's not the same kind of individualization in flowers that it is in man.

In flowers it's more fluid; it manifests as a force, as consciousness rather than individuality. Take the rose, for example; its great perfection of form, color and scent expresses an aspiration and a soul-giving. Look at a rose opening in the morning at the first touch of the sun. It is a magnificent self-giving in aspiration."

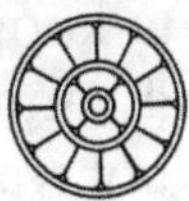

"Do flowers love? Yes, they do. This is their form of love, this blossoming. Certainly when one sees a rose opening to the sun, it is like a need to give its beauty. Only for us it is almost unintelligible, for they do not think about what they do.

A human being always associates everything he does with this ability to see himself doing it; that is, to think about himself – think of himself doing it. Man knows that he is doing something.

Animals don't think. It is not at all the same form of love.

Flowers, so to speak, are not conscious; it is a spontaneous movement, not a consciousness that is conscious of itself, not at all. But it is a great Force which acts through all that, the great universal Consciousness and the great Force of Universal Love which makes all things blossom in beauty."

Members of the Ashram who had never gardened before, began to work with flowers as part of their spiritual growth.

The Mother once gave a small cutting of the pomegranate flower plant, which she called "Divine Love" to an Ashramite who was working as an Ashram gardener. "Can we grow this", Mother asked. He thought for a moment, and said; "Yes, Mother, I think we can".

The Ashramite planted the small cutting, but nothing seemed to grow, and he began to have doubts. Someone told him that the Mother had taken a keen interest in the tiny plant, so he tried everything he could think of, but nothing he did seemed to help.

When the Mother came to know of his despair, she asked
that the little plant be brought and kept in a place where she
could see it every day. The pot was put in a place where The
Mother looked at it every time she passed by.

A few days later, new buds were seen and the small cutting
grew vigorously. Soon its roots filled the small pot, and Mother
asked the gardener to transplant it into a larger pot. It filled
one pot after another. Finally it was planted in the rockery at
the entrance to the main Ashram building, where it is now
full grown; the size of a small tree.

The coming of World War II in 1939 brought families with
children into the Ashram, and the atmosphere changed as
the Mother embraced them all, body, mind and soul. Some
children of visiting families refused to leave the Mother or
insisted on being brought back to the Mother. The Ashram
was full of flowers and children, and everything grew in the
Mother's wisdom and love. When the children were old
enough, she spoke to them about the value of their dreams.

"There is a world in which you are the supreme maker of
forms: that world is your own particular vital world. You are
the supreme fashioner and you can make a marvel of your
world if you know how to use it. If you have an artistic or
poetic consciousness, if you love harmony, beauty, you will
build there something marvelous which will tend to spring
up into the material manifestation.

When I was small I used to call this "telling stories to
oneself". It is not at all a telling with words, in one's head:
it is a going away to this place which is fresh and pure, and...

building up a wonderful story there. And if you know how to tell yourself a story in this way, and if it is truly beautiful, truly harmonious, truly powerful and well co-ordinated, this story will be realized in your life—perhaps not exactly in the form in which you created it, but as a more or less changed physical expression of what you made. That may take years, perhaps, but your story will tend to organise your life.

But there are very few people who know how to tell a beautiful story; and then they always mix horrors in it, which they regret later.

If one could create a magnificent story without any horror in it, nothing but beauty, it would have a considerable influence on everyone's life. And this is what people don't know.

If one knew how to use this power, this creative power in the world of vital forms, if one knew how to use this while yet a child, a very small child... for it is then that one fashions his material destiny. But usually people around you, sometimes even your own little friends, but mostly parents and teachers, dabble in it and spoil everything for you, so well that very seldom does the thing succeed completely.

But otherwise, if it were done like that, with the spontaneous candour of a child, you could organize a wonderful life for yourself—I am speaking of the physical world.

The dreams of childhood are the realities of mature age."

In 1943, the Mother opened the Ashram School which she said would be a center for the evolution of consciousness in body, mind and spirit. In 1945 she opened the Physical Education Department for the whole Ashram because physical education is the most effective tool to transform the body. Physical culture was used as the process of infusing the new consciousness into the cells to transform the body.

The Mother was the school's French teacher. Soon she was teaching the children in French about the work she and Sri Aurobindo were doing and the dawning of the new consciousness. All the Ashramites wanted to be wherever the Mother was, and soon everyone was in the Mother's class. She taught about the planes and parts of the human being, and she used a flower she called "Imagination" to explain different mental capacities.

"Imagination is something very complex and manifold—what is vaguely called "imagination".

Imagination can be the capacity for seeing, and for recording; for noting the forms in some mental or other domain. There are artistic, literary, poetic domains, domains of action, scientific domains, all belonging to the mind—not a very high and abstract mind, a mind above the physical mind which, without our knowing it, pours out constantly through the individual and collective mind to manifest in action.

Some people, through a special faculty, are in contact with these domains. They take up one formation or other that is there, draw these formations to themselves and give them an expression. This power of expression is different in different people, but those who can open themselves to these domains, to see things there, to draw these forms towards themselves and express them—either in literature or painting or music or in action or science—are, according to the degree of their power of expression, either very highly talented beings, or else geniuses.

There are higher geniuses still. They are people who can open to a higher region, a higher force which, passing through the mental layers, comes and takes a form in a human mind and reveals itself in the world as new truths, new philosophical systems, new spiritual teachings, which are the works and at the same time the actions of the great beings who come to take birth on earth. That is an imagination which can be called "Truthimagination".

These higher forces, when they come down into the earth-atmosphere, take living, active, powerful forms, spread throughout the world and prepare a new age.

These two kinds of imagination are what could be called higher imaginations. And now, to come down to a more ordinary level, everyone has in him, in a greater or lesser measure, the power to give form to his mental activity and use this form either in his ordinary activity or to create and realize something."

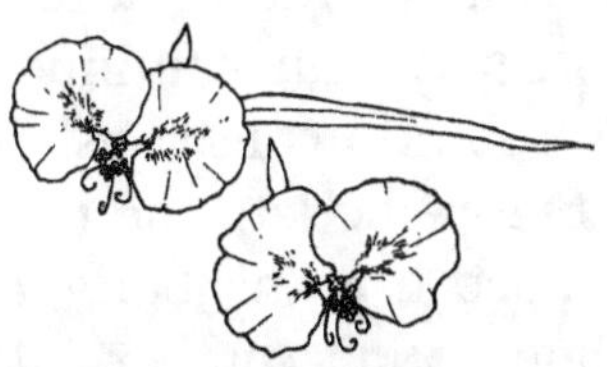

Starting in 1926, when Sri Aurobindo withdrew from outer life, Sri Aurobindo and the Mother gave Darshan three times a year to give the results of their inner work to the Ashramites. After 1939, it became four times a year.

"Darshan" means the inner sight which reveals the truth of the thing seen. The Darshan of a realized person imparts something of their spiritual realization. The Mother said these Darshans were the fulfillment of a great deal of work which had been done, and inner preparation was necessary to receive it. The disciples did their best to prepare as they waited eagerly for each Darshan Day.

In the very beginning, the disciples had time alone with Sri Aurobindo and the Mother. They sat side by side, and each person could kneel down between them. They would place their hand on the person's head. But very soon there were so many people that there wasn't enough time for kneeling. Sri Aurobindo and the Mother sat some distance back, and the Ashramites stood alone before them. Soon people from all over India and the world wrote for permission to come for Darshan. After twelve years, the line became so long that everyone had to pass in front of Sri Aurobindo and the Mother without stopping. Everyone who speaks of their experience speaks of the love and the light, the power and the peace they felt at the Darshans.

In 1950, at the age of 78, Sri Aurobindo saw that the work of bringing down the new supramental consciousness would go faster if he was no longer in his physical body. The Mother's physical body was stronger and could receive the new forces better, so she would stay and continue with the work in the physical. Sri Aurobindo consciously allowed himself to become fatally ill. Before he left, the new consciousness he had accumulated passed from his body into the Mother. Sri Aurobindo left his body on December 5, 1950. His body was placed in a shrine called the Samadhi in the center of the Ashram courtyard.

All the Ashram grieved at the loss of Sri Aurobindo's physical presence, but people could feel his consciousness still among them. The Mother explained that Sri Aurobindo had only left his physical body, and that his consciousness was firmly established in the earth's atmosphere, continuing their work of manifesting the new consciousness. Sri Aurobindo speaks of moving beyond life in a sonnet called "Cosmic Consciousness".

COSMIC CONSCIOUSNESS

I have wrapped the whole world in my wider self
    And Time and Space my spirit's seeing are.
I am the god and demon, ghost and elf,
    I am the wind's speed and the blazing star.

All Nature is the nursling of my care,
    I am the struggle and the eternal rest;
The world's joy thrilling runs through me, I bear
    The sorrow of millions in my lonely breast.

I have learned a close identity with all,
    Yet am by nothing bound that I become;
Carrying in me the universe's call
    I mount to my imperishable home.

I pass beyond time and life on measureless wings,
Yet still am one with born and unborn things. ✡

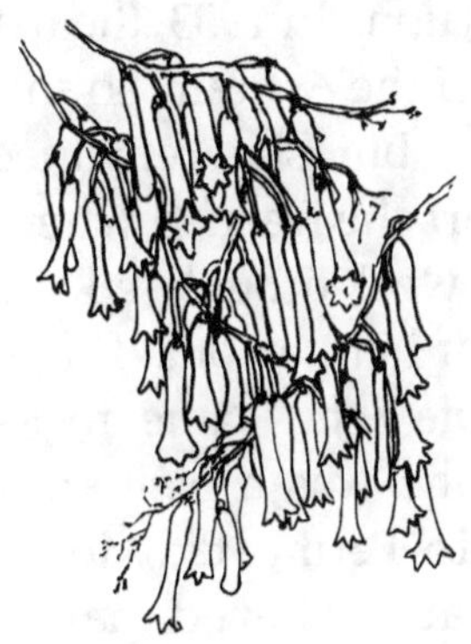

The Mother continued Sri Aurobindo's work of bringing consciousness into the earth's atmosphere and the cells of her own physical body. The Mother went on working with the children and the Ashramites. For twelve years the Mother gave Darshan alone, sitting in a chair opposite to the small Darshan room where she and Sri Aurobindo had given Darshan in the past. With all her added work, she continued running the Ashram.

The department heads wanted to be in her presence and to receive her wise guidance. They reported to her and referred the major decisions to her. The Ashram grew its own organic food, and from time to time, the Mother would visit outlying Ashram properties to see how things were progressing.

One day the Mother went to the Ashram Lake Estate to see the progress of the work going on there. As she was being shown around the property, she had to cross fields where wild flowers were growing. Mother stopped at the edge of a field, which was studded with tiny blossoms of all sorts of wild flowers. With a smile she asked; "But where can I put my foot"?

The Mother was still taking only two hours a night to retire on her couch in the salon. In 1953, the disciples constructed a room for her on top of the Ashram, so she could have privacy. She moved upstairs, but she remained physically active, playing tennis, a sport she learned when she was eight years old. As the Mother's work progressed, more and more people came from outside for her personal Darshan.

One of the people who came to see the Mother was Anandamoyi Ma. She was a well-known spiritual figure. Her name meant "Bliss Permeated Mother". She was always in a state of bliss. Many believed that she was a living form of the Infinite and Eternal. She said that her ecstatic states were part of an ongoing process which was not for the benefit of the body she was in, but for the benefit of everyone, drawing them forward like a magnet on their path to perfection. The Mother said that Anandamoyi Ma lived in the world of Satchidananda, pure existence, consciousness and bliss.

Anandamoyi Ma always traveled with a group of disciples. The Mother gave Anandamoyi Ma a special time in the morning to come to her room. Everyone thought that Anandamoyi Ma would meet the Mother alone, but they were told that all the disciples expected to go with her.

Anandamoyi Ma spoke Bengali. Mother didn't speak any Bengali. When the Mother was informed that Anandamoyi Ma spoke only Bengali, and that all of her disciples wanted to come, she said; "That's all right. Let them come. We will have no problem.

Anandamoyi Ma went up to the Mother's room with her disciples. She was there for about half an hour. She put her head on Mother's lap and went into deep trance.

Downstairs the Ashramites were waiting to hear about the conversation between these two great spiritual beings. After Anandamoyi Ma left, they asked Mother's attendants what the two of them said to each other. Mother's attendants said, "We can't tell you what they said because they didn't speak to each other".

The Mother's attendants related that Mother had kept flowers for Anandamoyi Ma on a small table next to her chair, and after Anandamoyi Ma put her head on the Mother's lap, Mother chose certain flowers for her. When the Mother gave her the flowers, Anandamoyi Ma took some of the flowers that Mother had given her, and gave them back to the Mother. Then the Mother gave Anandamoyi Ma some more flowers, and Anandamoyi Ma gave some more flowers back to Mother. The two of them were laughing, and they gave flowers back and forth to each other for quite a long time.

Mother's attendants said; "We don't know what happened. The two of them just went on giving flowers to each other".

In 1962 the Mother stopped all outside activities to stay in her room so she could devote herself to the inner work. She stopped giving public Darshans. All the Ashram longed for the Mother's Darshan, so in 1963, because of the Ashramites' need, she started coming out onto the terrace of the new room for Darshan four times a year. Now thousands of people gathered below her. Each person could feel the Mother looking at them.

Bathed in the Mother's love and the light of her consciousness, the Ashram continued to expand. The school flourished. Many children developed special capacities. The first children to come to the Ashram stayed on to become teachers themselves, or to work in the Ashram Departments.

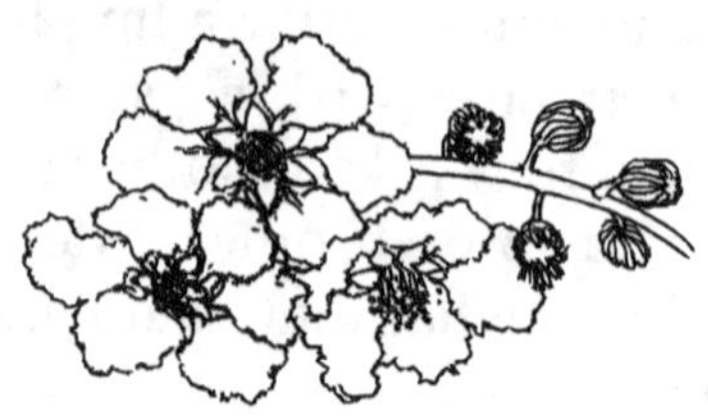

There was a young lady in the Ashram who had the gift of seeing nature spirits and fairies. The Mother encouraged her to develop her gift, and she wrote many fairy stories.

This Ashramite married and had a daughter. When the little girl started kindergarten in the Ashram school, she heard many fairy tales, and she began to develop an interest in fairies, so at home the little girl's mother read to her and told her many fairy stories. Soon the child was saying that she wanted to see fairies.

In those days, many Ashramites were able to see the Mother on a regular basis. This lady and her daughter saw the Mother on Sunday afternoons. One Sunday the little girl told the Mother that she wanted to see a fairy. The Mother was very pleased, and gave her a lot of encouragement, telling her that if she really wanted to see fairies, she could certainly see them. The little girl said again, "I want to see a fairy", and Mother said; "Ask your mother. She will show them to you, because she sees them all the time".

The Ashramite was completely taken aback - what was the Mother doing? To see and feel fairies oneself was one thing, but to show them to someone else? This was quite a different thing. The Mother was watching her obvious feelings of insecurity and her expression of reluctance and dismay.

There was a tray of flowers on a small table next to the Mother's chair. On the tray were some small lilies, commonly called "Fairy Lily" or "Rain Lily". The Mother called these flowers "Prayer". Picking up two Prayer flowers, a yellow one and a white one, the Mother gave them to the Ashramite and her daughter, saying to both of them; "With the help of these flowers, you will be able to see fairies". Carefully holding the small lilies, they walked home in quiet of the late afternoon.

The Ashramite had told her own child that fairies were real, and she felt deeply the responsibility that the Mother had given her, but she had no idea what she was supposed to do. When they arrived home, she put the Prayer flowers in front of the Mother's photograph and prayed with all her heart that her little daughter would see a fairy. She told the child that they would just sit and look at the flowers until something came out.

Sitting there, in an attitude of prayer, very concentrated in mind and spirit, trying to know what to do when the Mother had promised her daughter that she would show her a fairy, the Ashramite started to speak, almost automatically; "The fairy might wear her anklet, and if you remain very quiet before she comes out, you might hear the tiny tinkling sound her anklet makes. Watch carefully, because she may not remain for a long time".

Then the child said; "There's a white one.......and there's a yellow one." Then she said; "Mummy, she's gone."

Many different kinds of flowers grew in the Ashram. People brought plants and seeds from all over the world. Greenhouses grew special flowers. More flowers were brought to the Mother to learn their true significance. Mother was asked to give comments on each flower, and the first flower book was published. Other books would follow in later years, and with the advent of computers, websites have been created, giving the world free access to the Mother's flower teachings.

When The Mother was 90 years old, one of her long-held dreams became a reality. She started an International city about 12 kilometers from the Ashram. It would be a place for people from all over the world to live together and work for human unity. She called the city "Auroville", City of Dawn. Auroville was inaugurated on February 28, 1968, and the earth from 121 countries was mingled in an urn at the city center.

Early pioneers came to the wide red earth under the vast blue sky. Mostly from Europe and North America, they felt they were coming home. They joined together in the most basic of living conditions to start building the Mother's vision of a new and better world. Because of the lack of modern conveniences and tools and building materials, they had to live and work closely together in order to survive and build; and thus began the serious practice of human unity which would involve every aspect of their lives.

They started to build the Matrimandir, a place for inner concentration, at the very center of Auroville. The Mother saw the inner chamber of the Matrimandir in a vision. She said The Matrimandir would be the soul of Auroville.

Drawn by the presence of the Mother and her work for a better world, more and more people came. Although the Mother was 12 kilometers away in the Ashram, the Aurovilians always felt the living presence of her love and care. They worked for a better world by working within themselves while they built the city of the future.

The Mother said that Auroville would be the cradle of the new man as the new consciousness became more available on earth. She said that Auroville would be the link with the outside world, and from all over the world, people came.

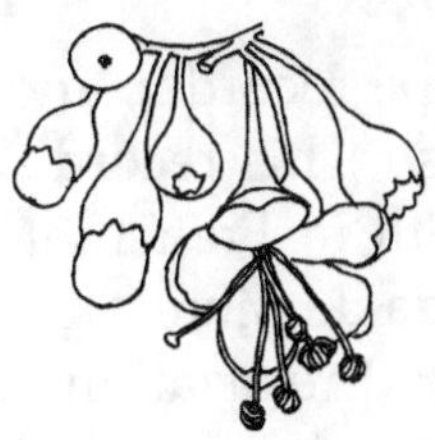

In 1973, a young woman who had recently spent some time in Auroville and the Ashram went to visit the Findhorn Community in the North-East of Scotland. The Mother had given her a blessing packet containing some rose petals charged with her force. Following the custom in those days, the young woman put the rose petals in an amulet which she wore around her neck for spiritual protection.

While she was in Findhorn, she loaned her amulet to a member of the Findhorn Community. He wore it around his neck for a few days, and during this period, he went rock climbing on the sandstone sea cliffs a few miles down the coast from Findhorn. He was high up on the cliff face when the piece of rock he was holding on to broke, and he plummeted thirty feet straight down to land flat on his chest on the rocky ground directly below him.

According to the laws of nature, he should have been badly hurt, with broken ribs and other serious injuries, but because he was wearing the rose petals which the Mother had charged with her force, he was virtually unharmed.

It was only when he returned the amulet to the young woman, two days after his fall, that his ribs first started to feel sore.

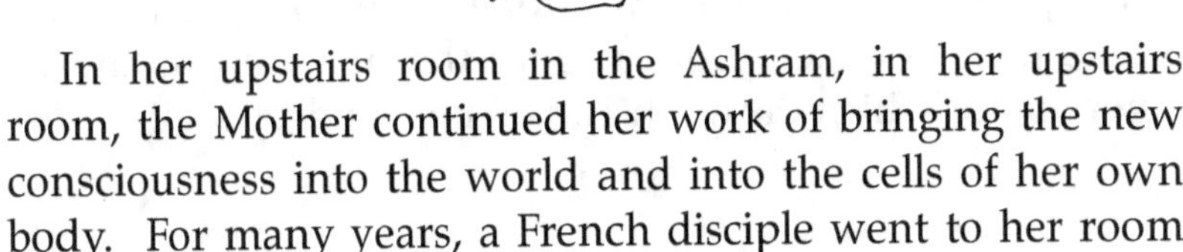

In her upstairs room in the Ashram, in her upstairs room, the Mother continued her work of bringing the new consciousness into the world and into the cells of her own body. For many years, a French disciple went to her room twice a week with a tape recorder, and the Mother spoke of her work and progress. This record of the Mother's work has been published both in French and English in thirteen volumes titled "L'Agenda de Mere", "Mother's Agenda". The Mother's experiences and realizations give us guideposts on our way to the next step in human evolution.

On November 17, 1973, at the age of 95, after having reached a stage where she had done all the earth could bear up to that point in time, the Mother withdrew from her physical body. She left a legacy of love and wisdom which sustains and guides growing numbers of people. Like Sri Aurobindo, although her body is in the Samadhi in the main Ashram courtyard, her universalized consciousness continues to work in the earth's atmosphere. Countless people still relate experiences of Mother and Sri Aurobindo's living presence and their help and guidance.

One of the sweetest gifts the Mother has given to the earth and her children is the teachings of flowers. She has given us the living earth to be our teacher. As the new consciousness continues to manifest here, we are partly an artisan of our own change. Our conscious will and participation are part of the journey on the pathways opened by the Mother and Sri Aurobindo which bring us into the new and unknown dawning for which the earth and all her children wait.

REMINISCENCE

My soul arose at dawn and, listening, heard
One voice abroad, a solitary bird,
A song not master of its note, a cry
That persevered into eternity.
My soul leaned out into the dawn to hear
In the world's solitude its winged compeer
And, hearkening what the Angel had to say,
Saw lustre in midnight and a secret day
Was opened to it. It beheld the stars
Born from a thought and knew how being prepares.
Then I remembered how I woke from sleep
And made the skies, built earth, formed Ocean deep.

REFERENCES

The passages in this book have been selected from the following publications:

Collected Works of Sri Aurobindo: (CWSA).

Collected Works of The Mother: (CWM).

P.1   FLOWERS AND THEIR MESSAGES, 1995 ED. PP. VIII, IX

P.3   QUESTIONS AND ANSWERS 1929-1931, CWM, VOL. 3, P.132

P.3   QUESTIONS AND ANSWERS 1954, CWM, VOL. 6, PP. 229-30

P.5   QUESTIONS AND ANSWERS 129-1931, CWM, VOL. 3, PP. 72-3

P.7, QUESTIONS AND ANSWERS 1950-1951, CWM, VOL. 4, P. 167

P.8   QUESTIONS AND ANSWERS 1929-1931, CWM, VOL. 3, P. 168

P.9   QUESTION AND ANSWERS 1956, CWM, VOL. 8, PP. 399-400

P.11 SRI AUROBINDO COLLECTED POEMS, CWSA, VOL. 2, P. 625

P.12 SRI AUROBINDO COLLECTED POEMS, CWSA, VOL. 2, P. 623

P.13 QUESTION AND ANSWERS, 1929-1931, CWM, VOL. 3, P. 130

P.15 SRI AUROBINDO COLLECTED POEMS, CWSA, VOL. 2, P. 623

P.16 FLOWERS AND THEIR MESSAGES, P. 260

P.20 FLOWERS AND THEIR SPIRITUAL SIGNIFICANCE, P. 30

P.21 FLOWERS AND THEIR MESSAGES, 1995 ED. P. VII

P.22 QUESTIONS AND ANSWERS 1950-1951, CWM, VOL. 4, P. 166-7

P.23 QUESTION AND ANSWERS 1953, CWM, VOL. 5, P. 243

P.24 QUESTION AND ANSWERS 1956, CWM, VOL. 8, PP. 118-19

P.26 QUESTIONS AND ANSWERS 1957-1958, CWM, VOL.9, PP. 385-386

P.28 SRI AUROBINDO COLLECTED POEMS, CWSA, VOL. 2, P. 603

P.37 SRI AUROBINDO COLLECTED POEMS, CWSA, VOL. 2, P. 203

FLOWERS

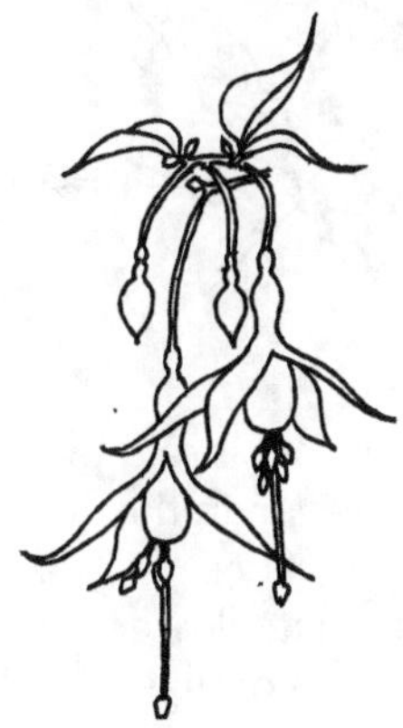

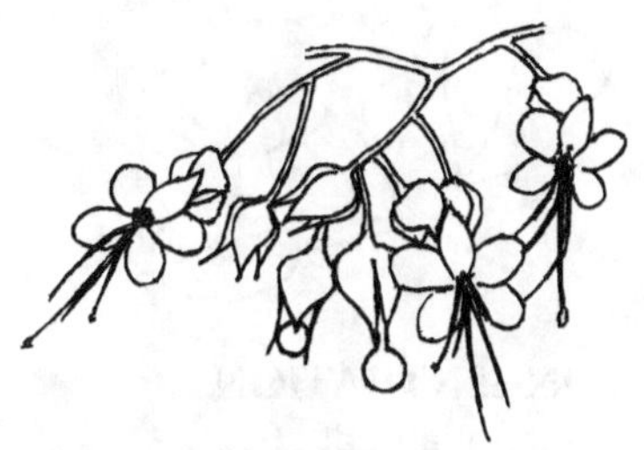

**ASPIRATION FOR
THE RIGHT ATTITUDE**
Energetic, willing, determined.
*Clerodendrum xspeciosum, Pagoda
flower*, java glory bean
Red, white calyx

ART
Living only to express beauty.
Fuchsia, Lady's-eardrops
Several colors

**AWAKENING AND FIRST
RESPONSE OF NATAURE
TO THE SUPRAMENTAL**
Interested, she opens herself
and tries to understand.
Jatropha integerrima,
Peregrina, Spicy jatropha
Reddish pink

**ASPIRATION IN THE PHYSICAL
FOR DIVINE LOVE**
Manifold, ecstatic, difficult to satisfy.
Russelia equisetiformis,
Coral plant, Fountain plant
Bright coral

CHARITY
Simple and Sweet,
attentive to the needs
of all.
Commalina. Dayflower
Sky blue

CONCENTRATION

Does not aim at effect,
but is simple and persistent.
Euphorbiamilii,
Crown of thorns,
Bright Red

DIVINE LOVE

A flower that is said to
blossom even in the desert.
Punica granatum.
Pomegranate flower
Orange red double

INTIMACY WITH UNIVERSAL NATURE

This intimacy is possible only for
those who are vast and without
preferences or repulsions.
Lagerstroemia speciosa, Crepe myrtle
Rose purple

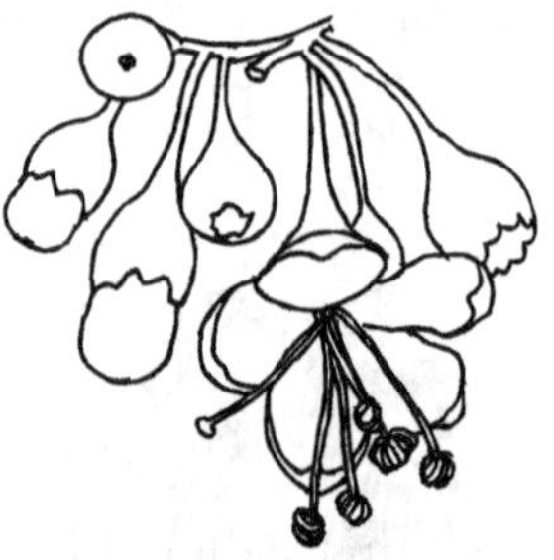

MATERIAL ENTERPRISES

Many Projects, Many
Attempts, Many Constructions
Ceiba pendantra. Kapok tree,
White silk-cotton tree
Cream White

NATURE MAKES AN OFFERING OF HER BEAUTY

It is a spontaneous and effortless offering.
Ipomoea, Morning glory, Many colors

OFFERING

The only offering that
enriches is the one that
is made to the divine.
Alcea rosea. Hollyhock
Many colors

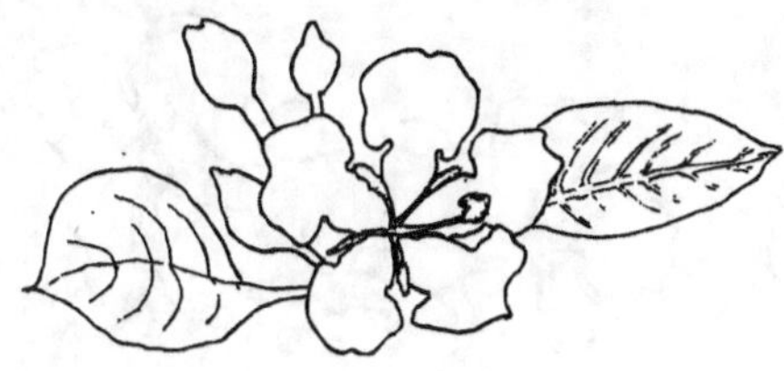

ORDER
To put each thing in its place
gives it its true value.
Randia Speciosa, Rubia,
Cream white

PURIFIED SENSES
Can only be obtained by a total
surrender to the truth.
Clitoria ternatea, Mussel-shell
creeper, White

STABILITY IN THE VITAL
One of the important results of
conversion.
Bauhinia purpurea,
Butterfly tree, Orchid tree
Light pink to reddish violet

PERFECT NEW CREATION
Clustered, complete, manifold,
it affirms its right to be.
Polianthes tuberose. Tuberose
White, double

SINCERITY IN THE VITAL
The sure way to realization.
Aster amelus, Aster
Lavender blue

SUCCESSFUL
FUTURE UNDER THE
SUPRAMENTAL INFLUENCE
(No comment)
Gallardia pulchella. Blanket
flower
Red and yellow

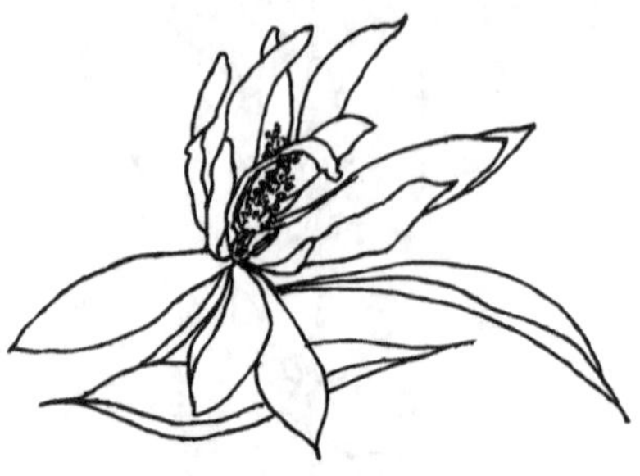

SUPRAMENTALISED PSYCHOLOGICAL PERFECTION

A psychological perfection aspiring to be divinized.
Michelia champaka, Champa
Cream yellow to golden orange

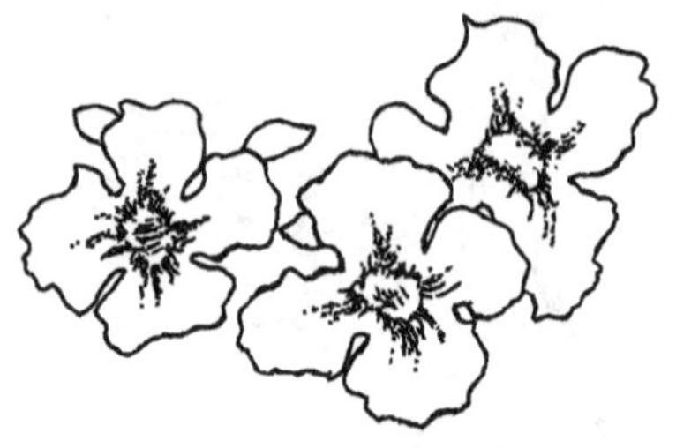

TO KNOW HOW TO LISTEN

To be attentive and silent.
Podranea ricasoliana, Pink trumpet vine
Light pink to lavender pink

TO LIVE ONLY FOR THE DIVINE

This means to have overcome all the difficulties of individual life.
Myrtus communis, Myrtle, White

TRANSFORMATION

The goal of creation.
Millingtonia hortensis.
Indian cork tree
White

VITAL OPENING

The vital is ready to receive the divine influence.
Saritaea magnifica
Rose Purple

www.ingramcontent.com/pod-product-compliance
Lightning Source LLC
Chambersburg PA
CBHW070610160726
48003CB00005B/2198